Claude Monet

Paintings

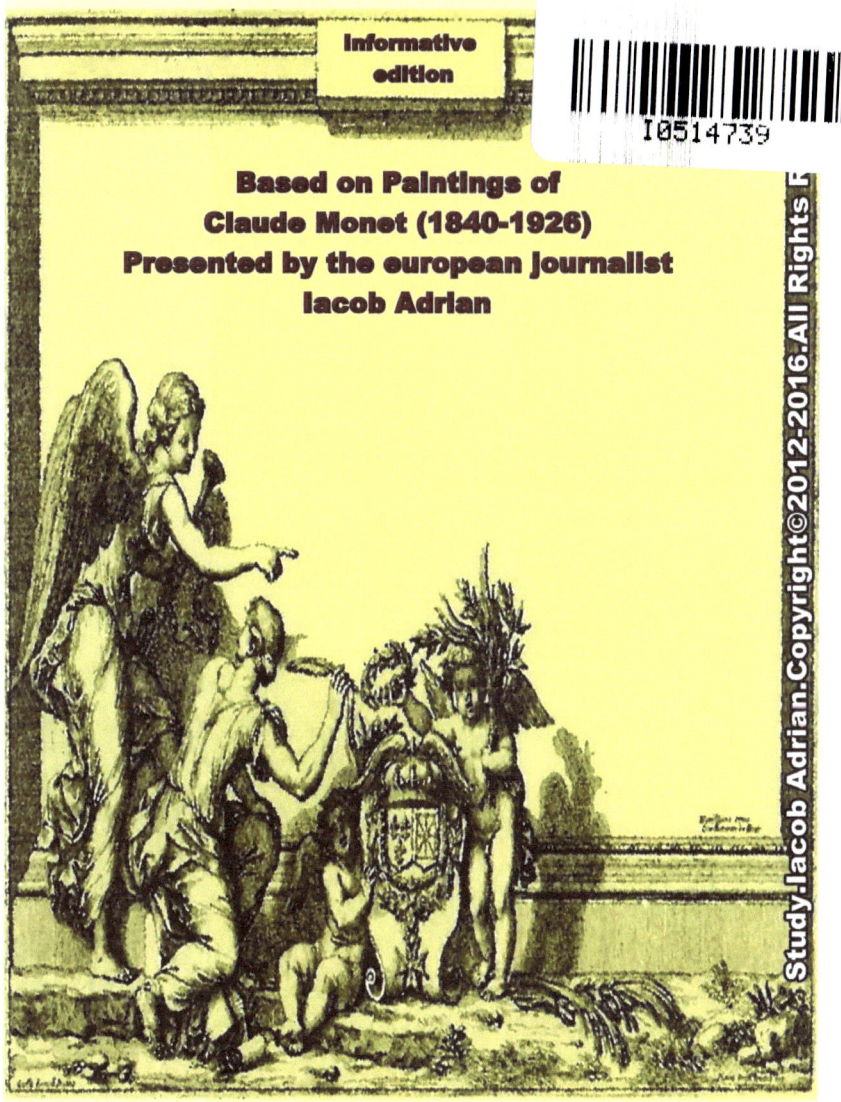

informative edition

**Based on Paintings of
Claude Monet (1840-1926)
Presented by the european journalist
Iacob Adrian**

ISBN-13 : 978-1974637836 -- ISBN-10 : 1974637832

Notice

This documentary study use historic, archived documents. Because of this, some pages may look blurry or low quality. Still are included in this book because they have high value from critical, documentary, historical, informative and journalistic point of view .

Dtp and visual art
Iacob Adrian

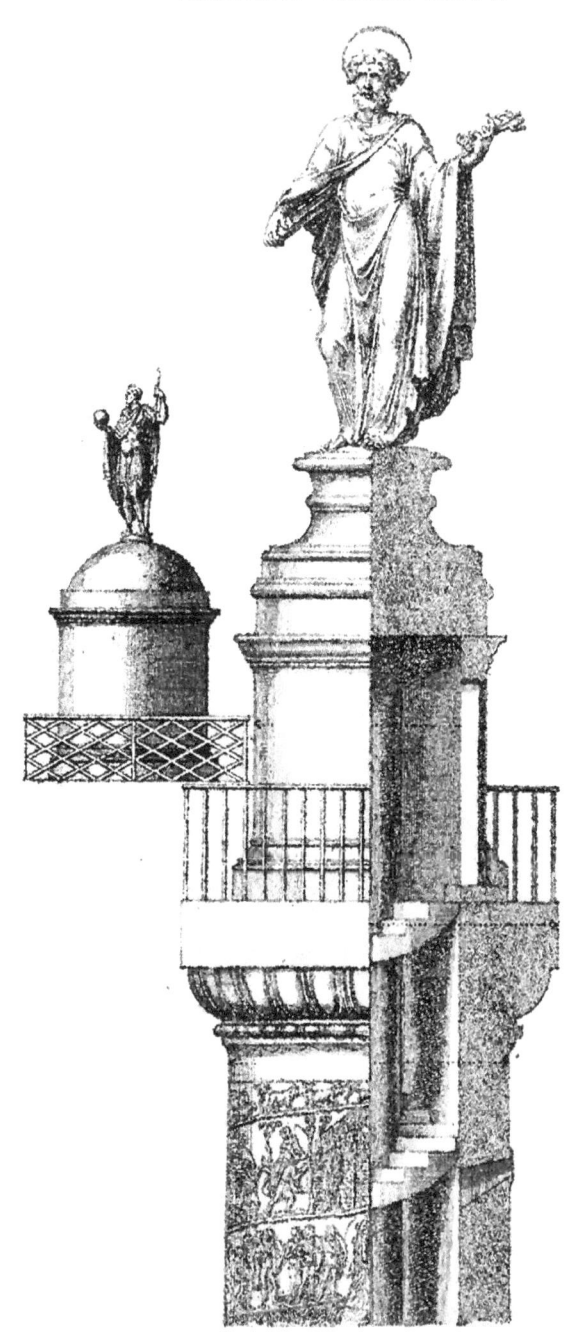

Editor
Iacob Adrian

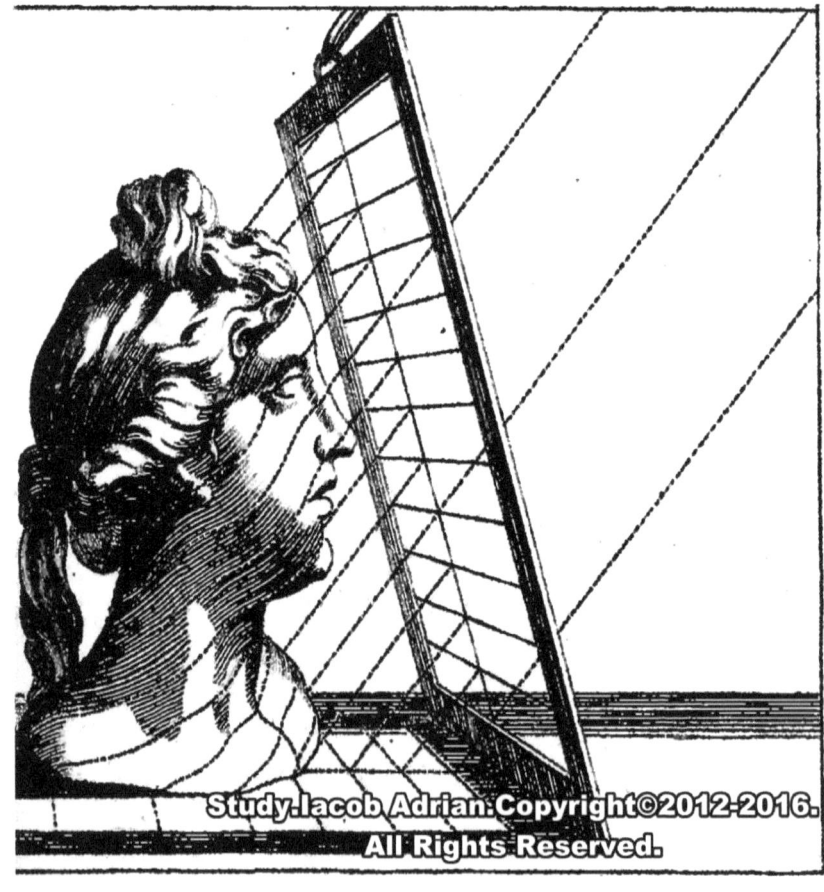

Editor statement

This is a series of classic books from classical authors .

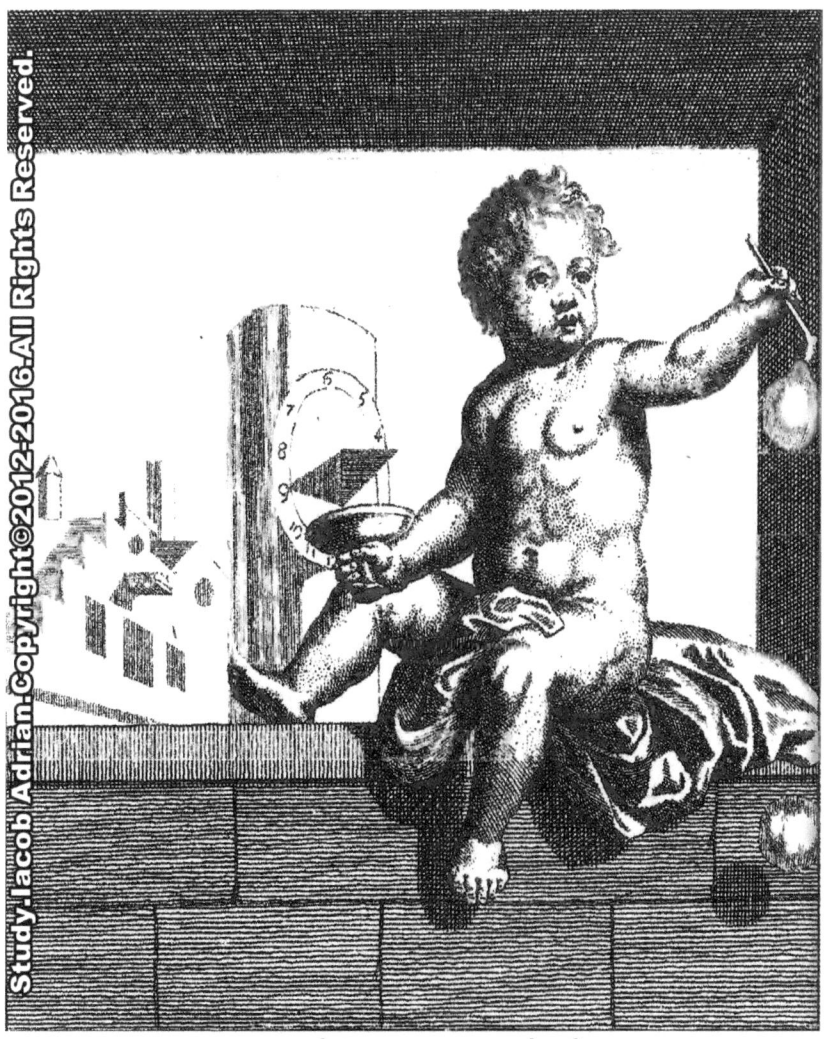

Copyright©2012-2016 Iacob Adrian
All Rights Reserved.

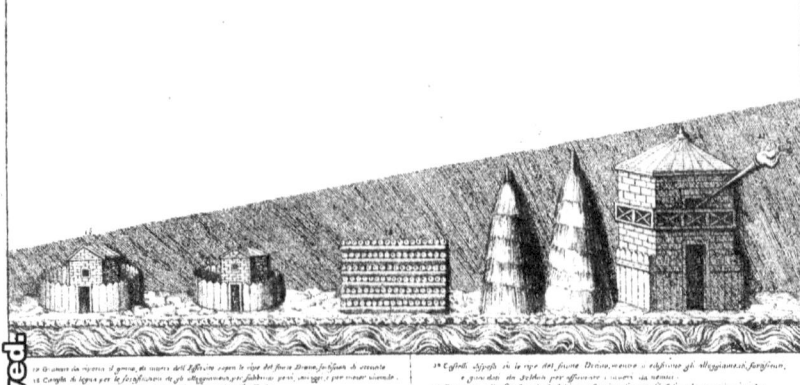

This little Book conveys the greetings of

....

to

....

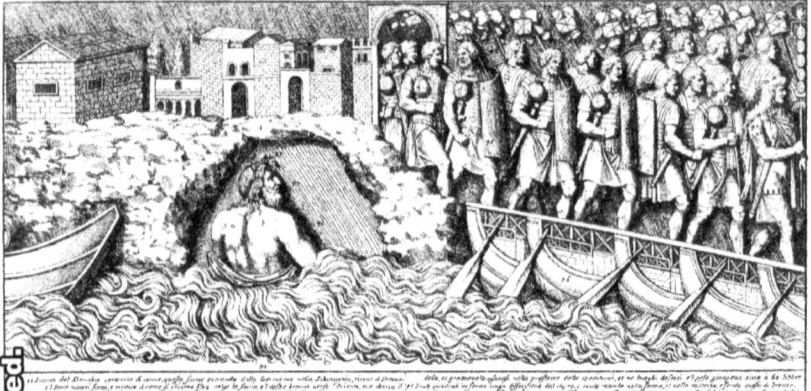

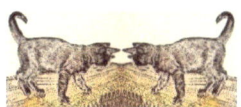

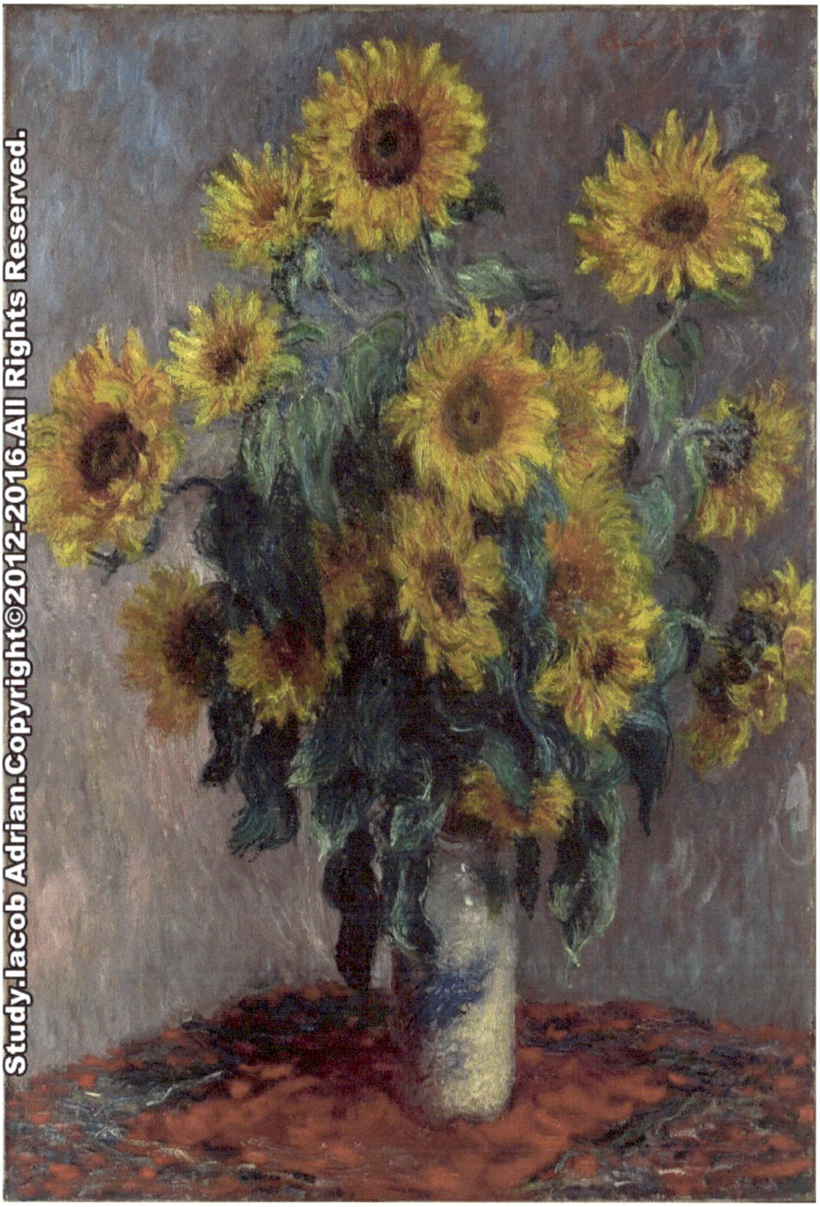

Bouquet of Sunflowers
Date : 1881

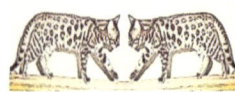

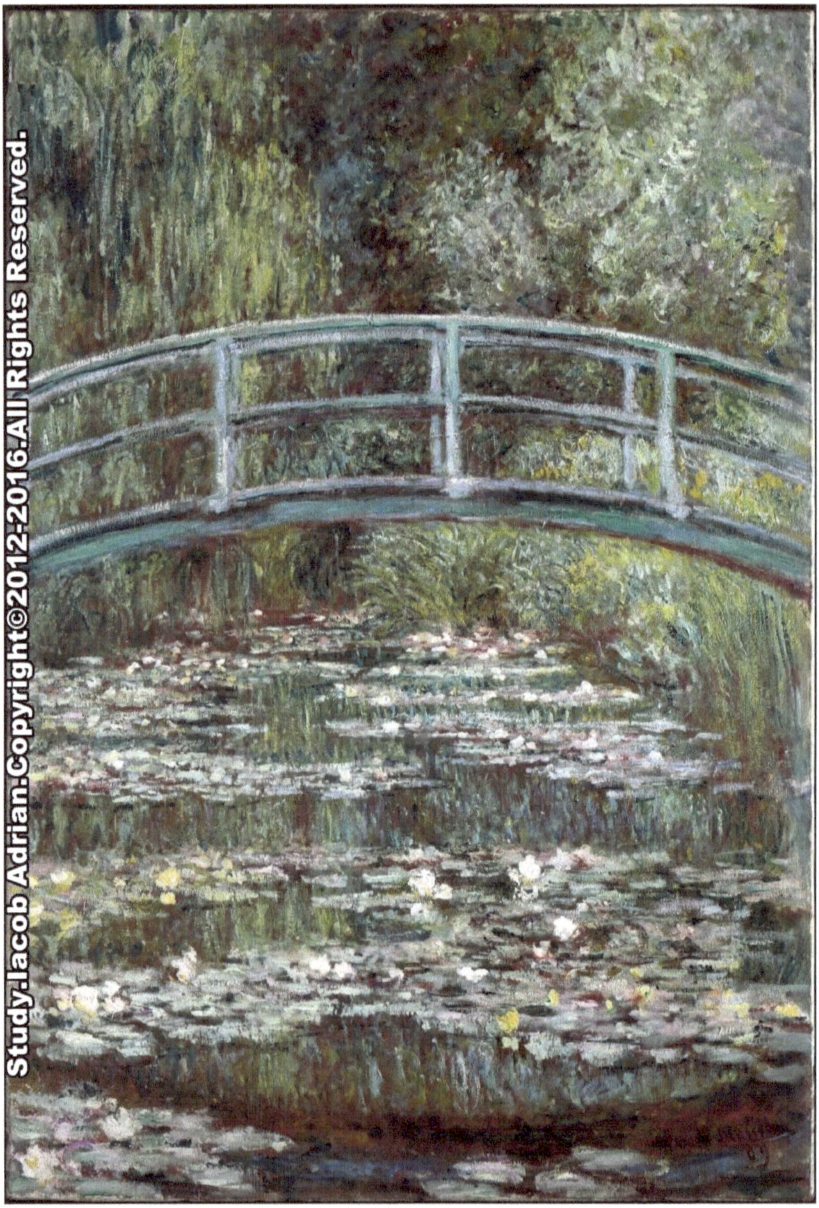

Bridge over a Pond of Water Lilies
Date : circa 1899

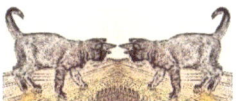

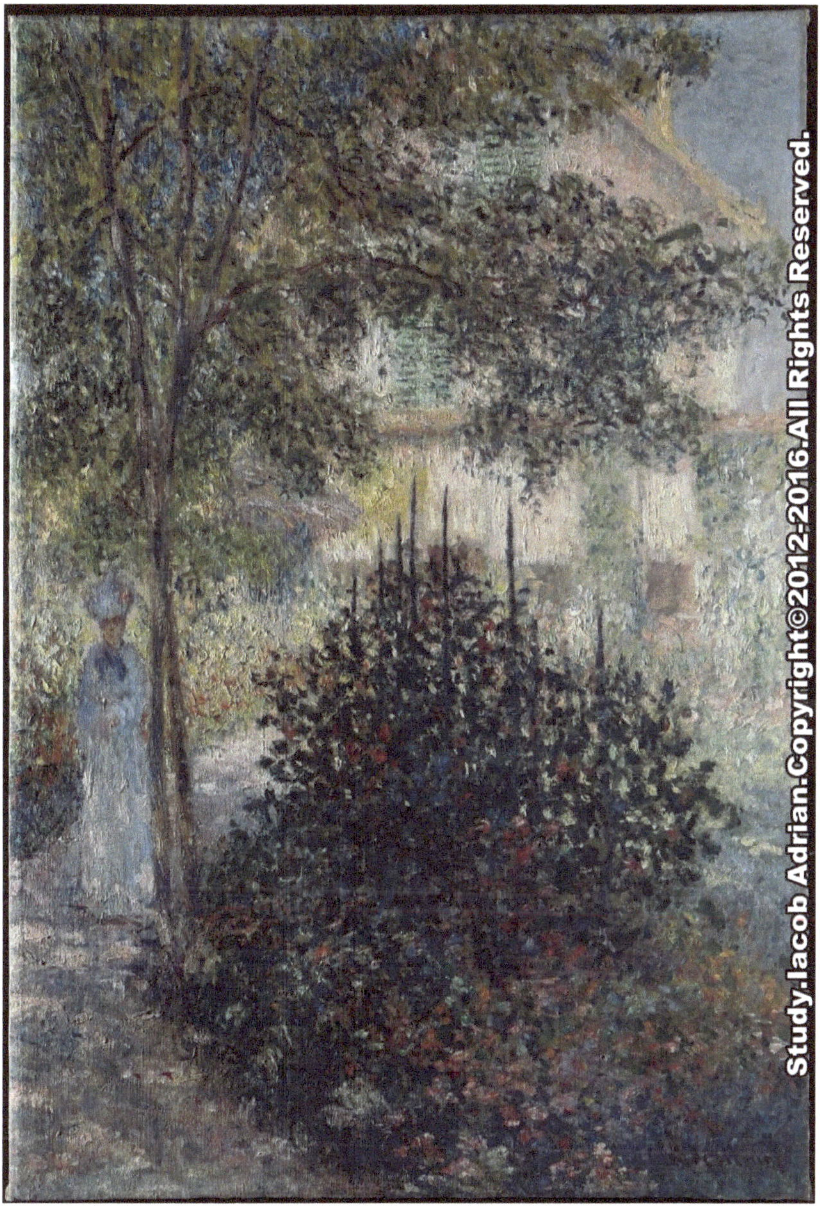

Camille Monet (1847–1879) in the Garden at Argenteuil
Date : 1876

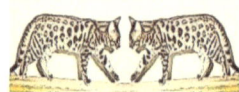

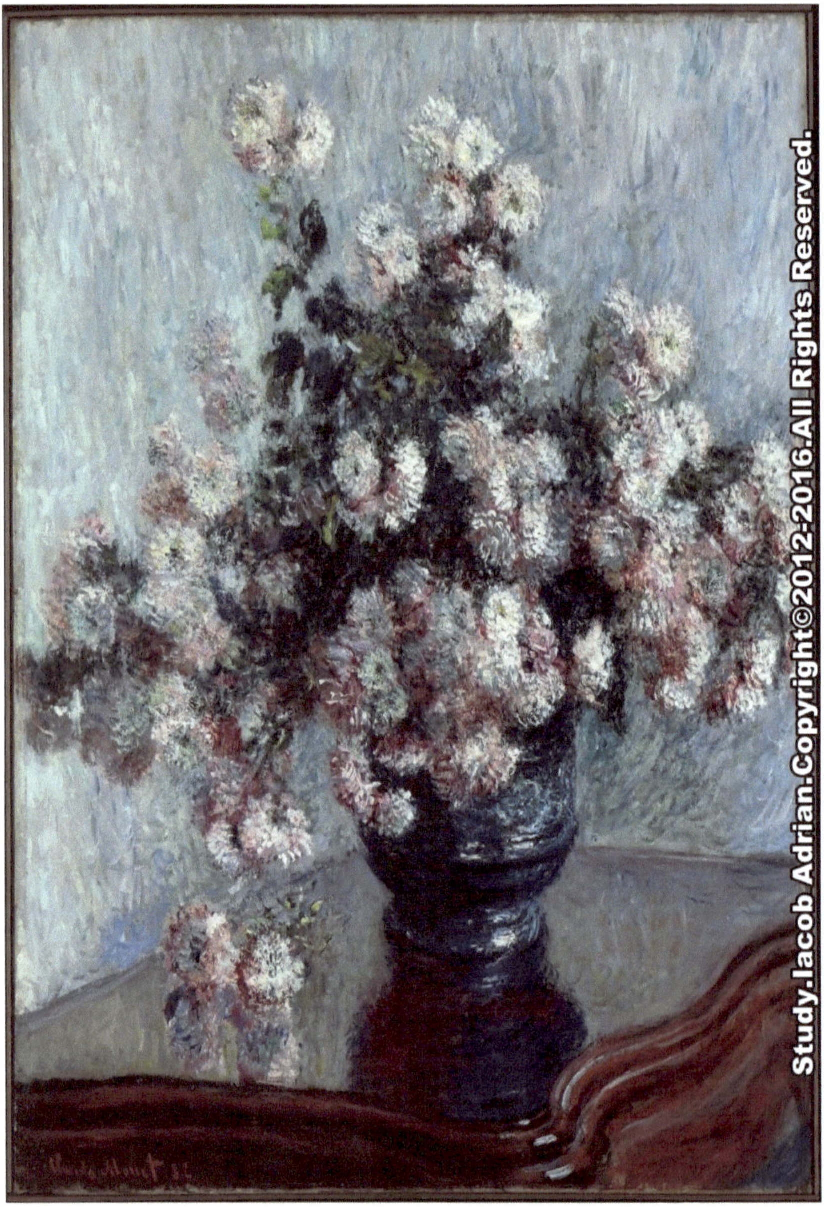

Chrysanthemums
Date : 1882

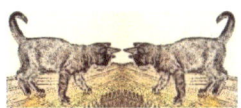

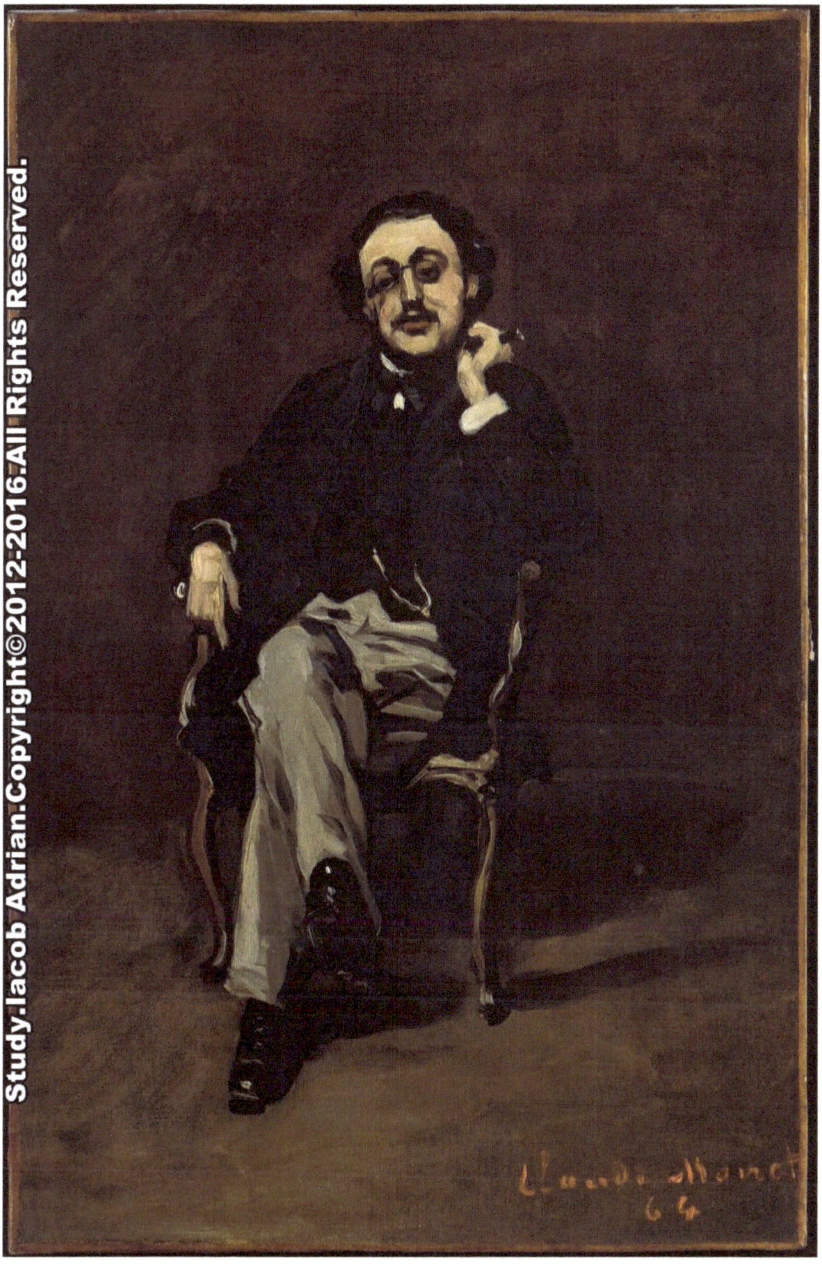

Dr. Leclenché
Date : 1864

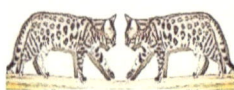

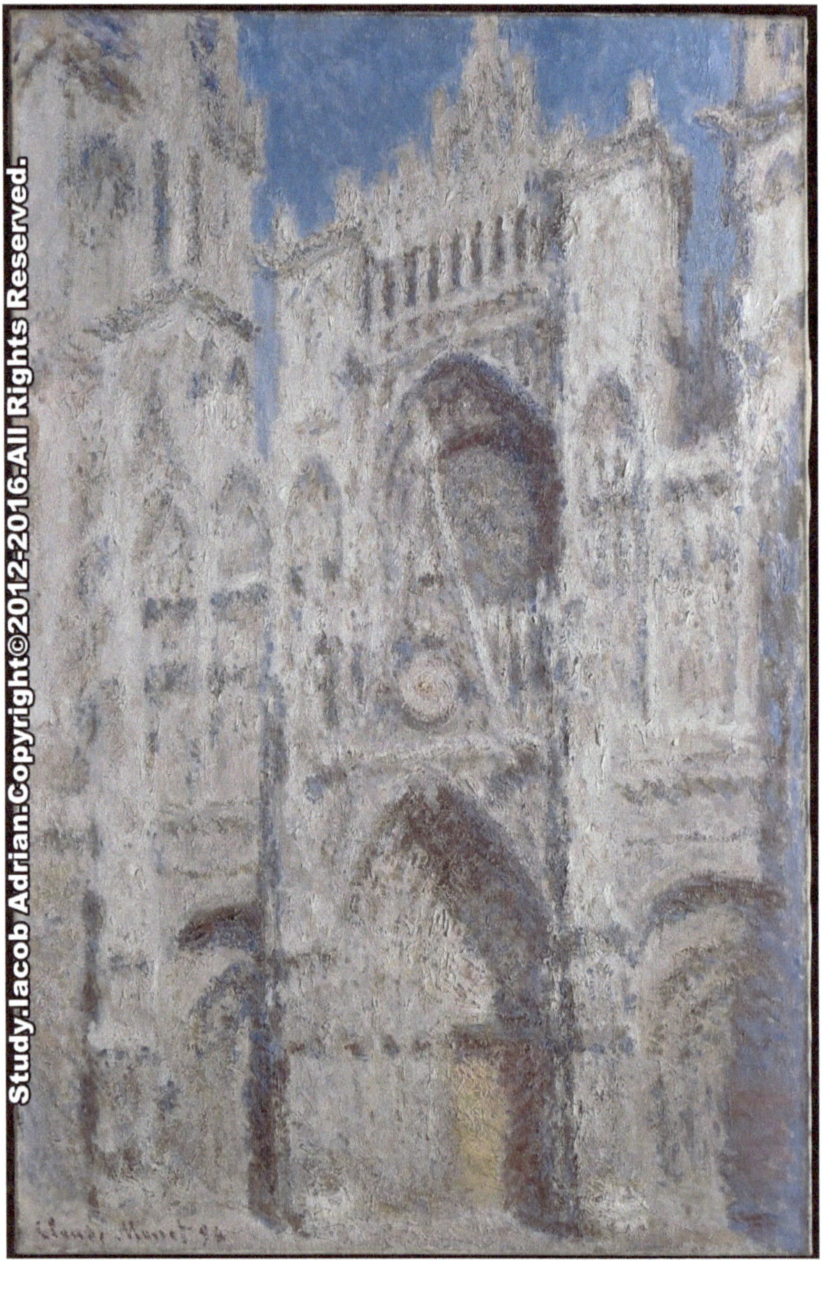

Rouen Cathedral: The Portal (Sunlight)
Date : 1894

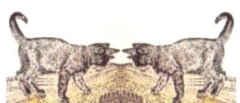

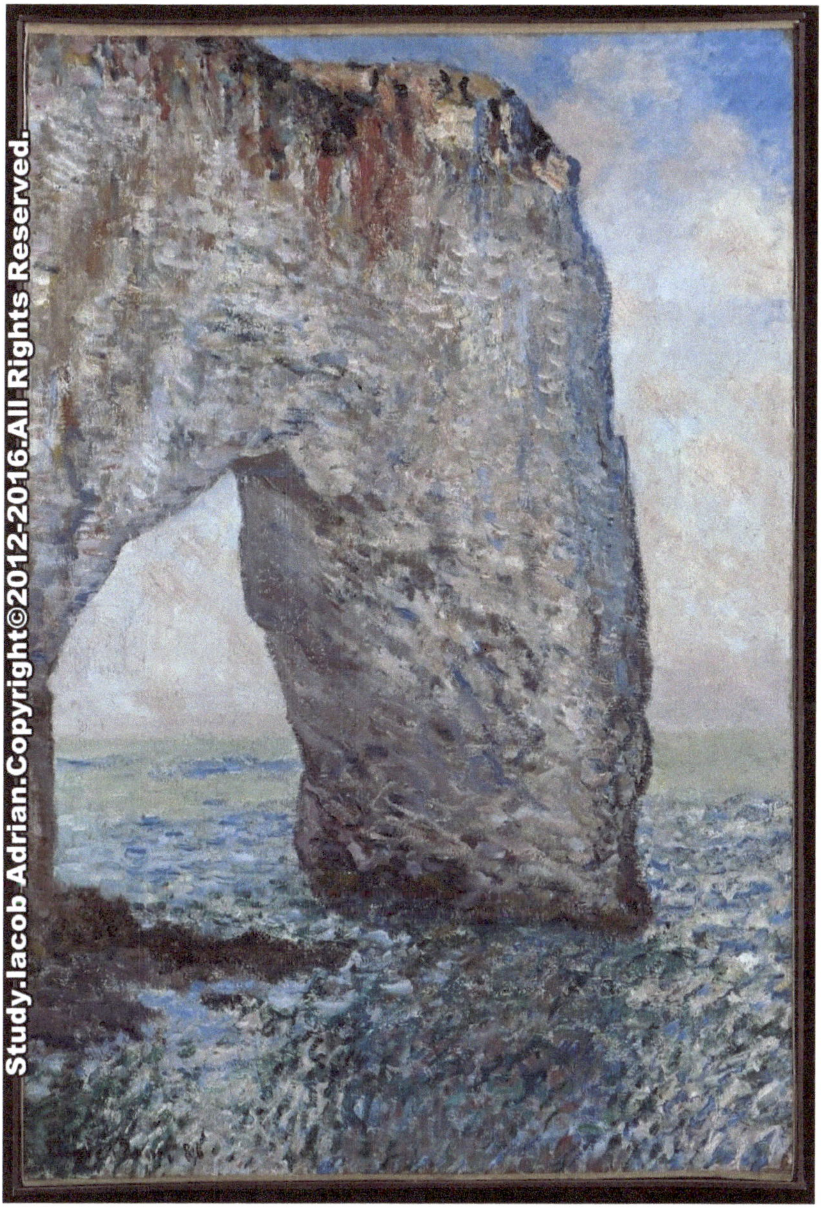

The Manneporte near Étretat
Date : 1886

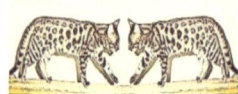

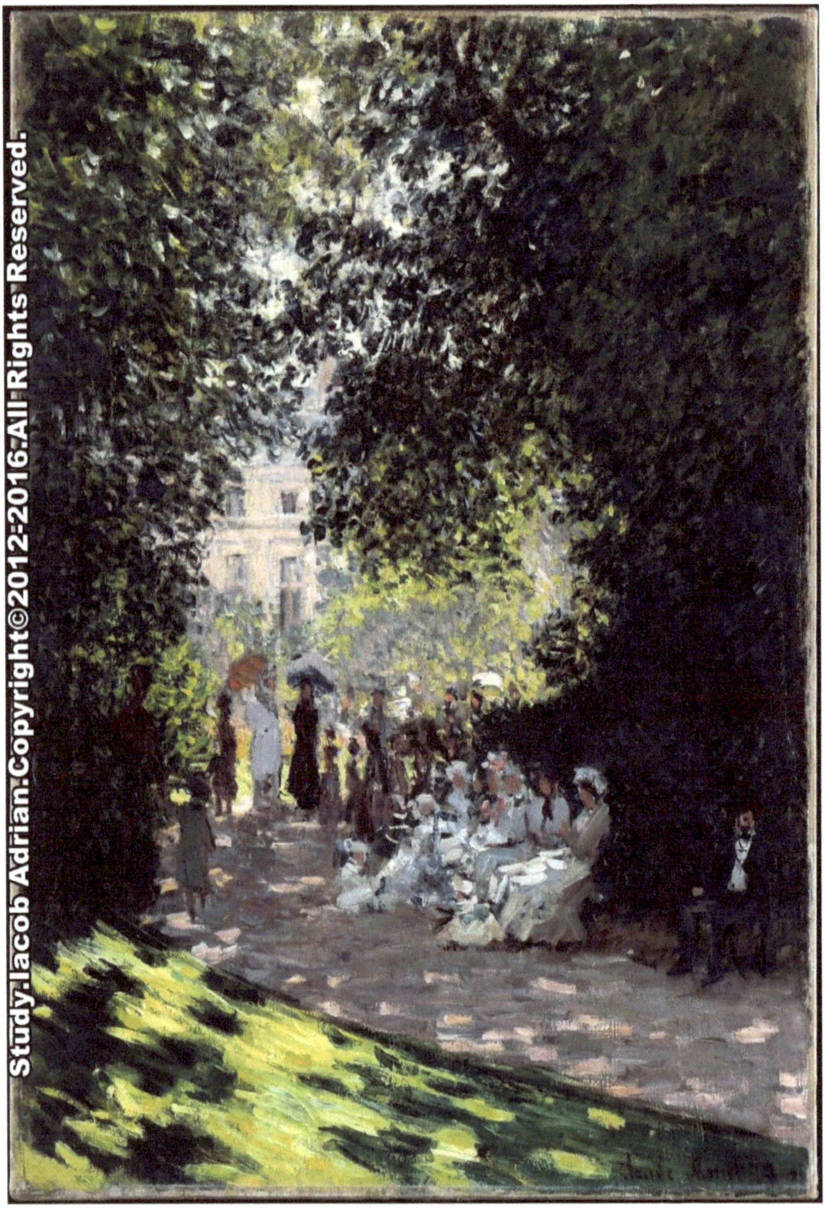

The Parc Monceau
Date : 1878

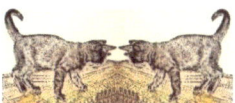

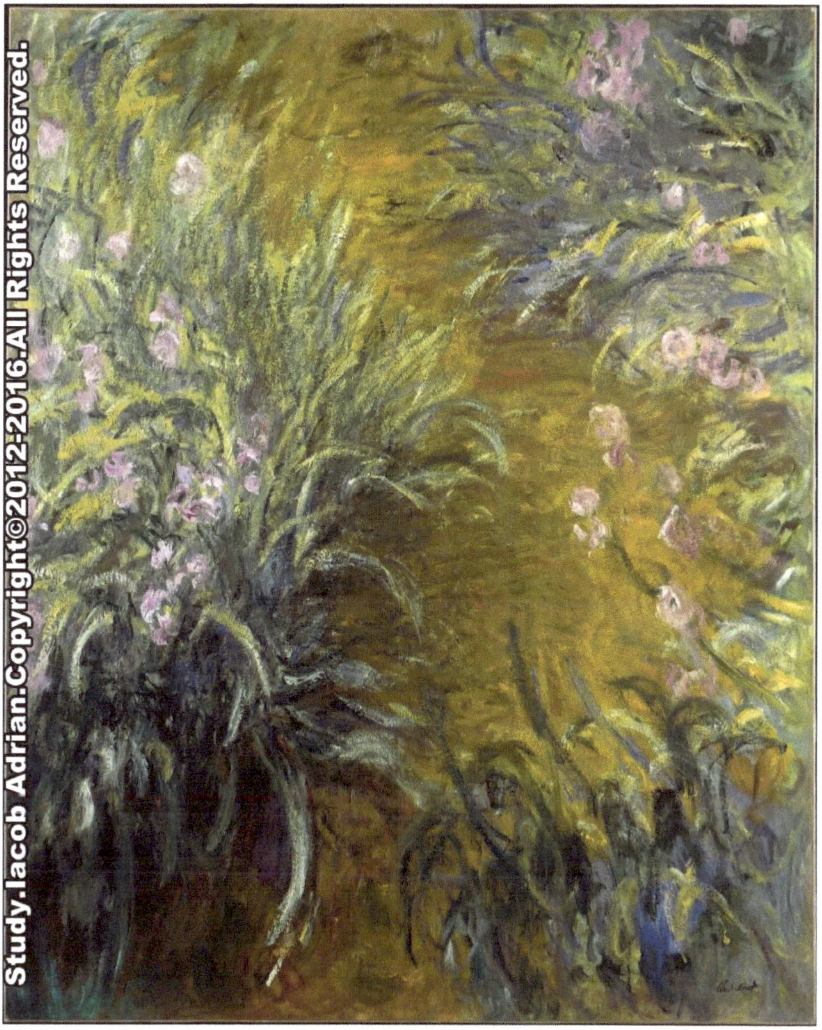

The Path through the Irises
Date : 1914–1917

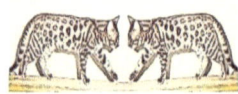

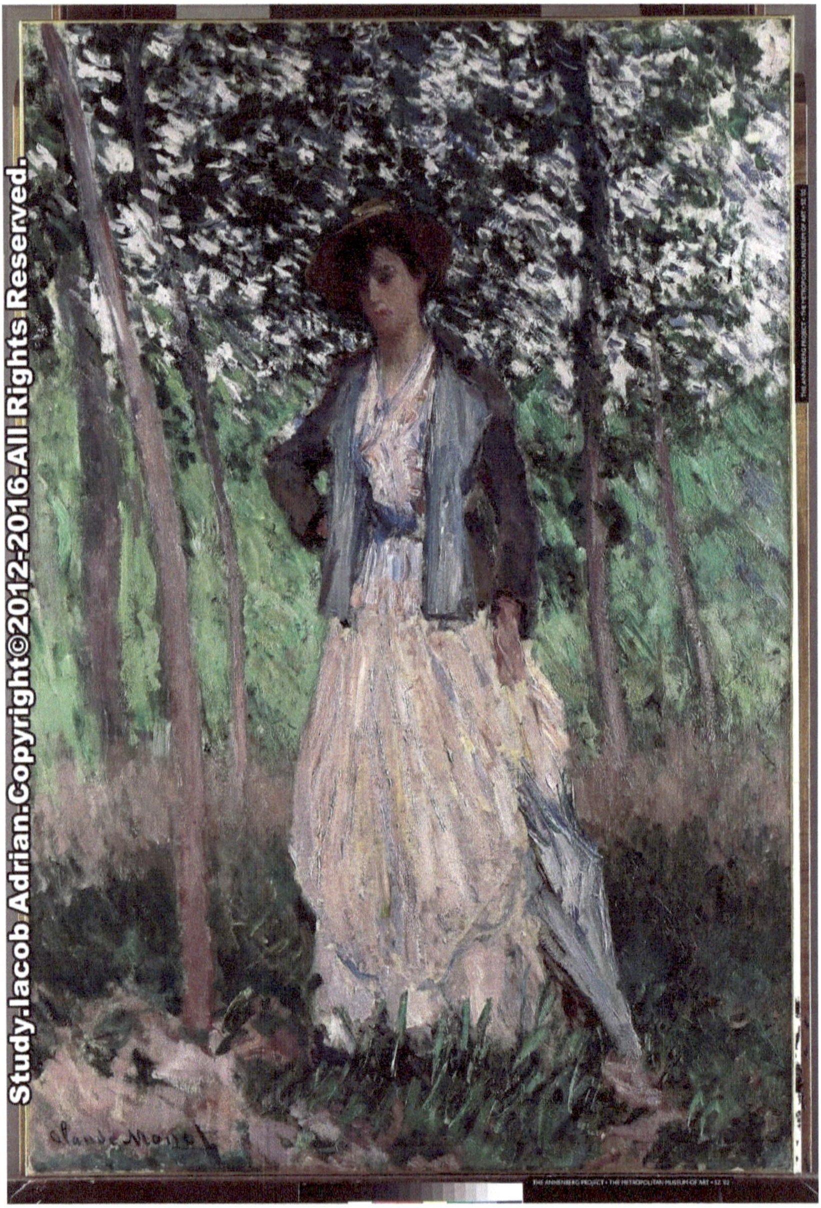

The Stroller (Suzanne Hoschedé, later Mrs. Theodore Earl Butler, 1868–1899)
Date : 1887

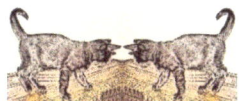

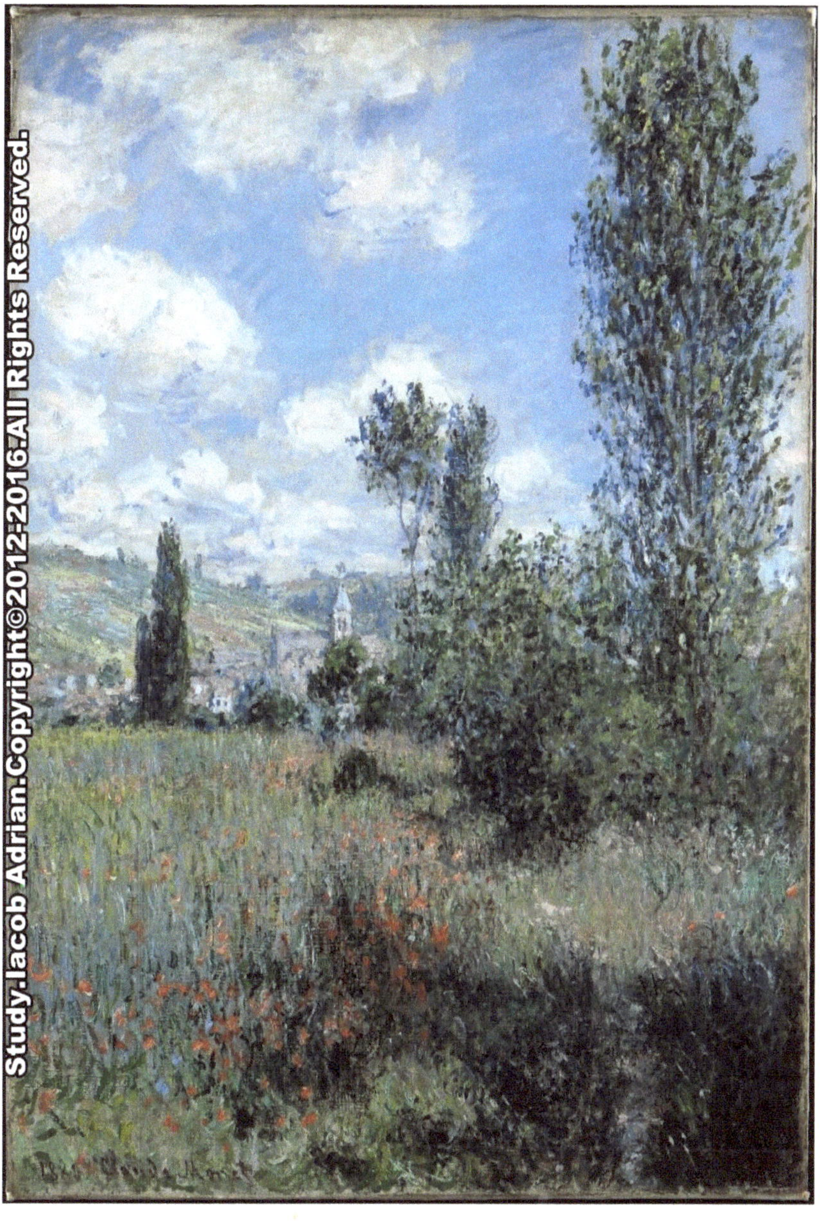

View of Vétheuil
Date : 1880

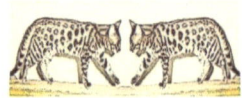

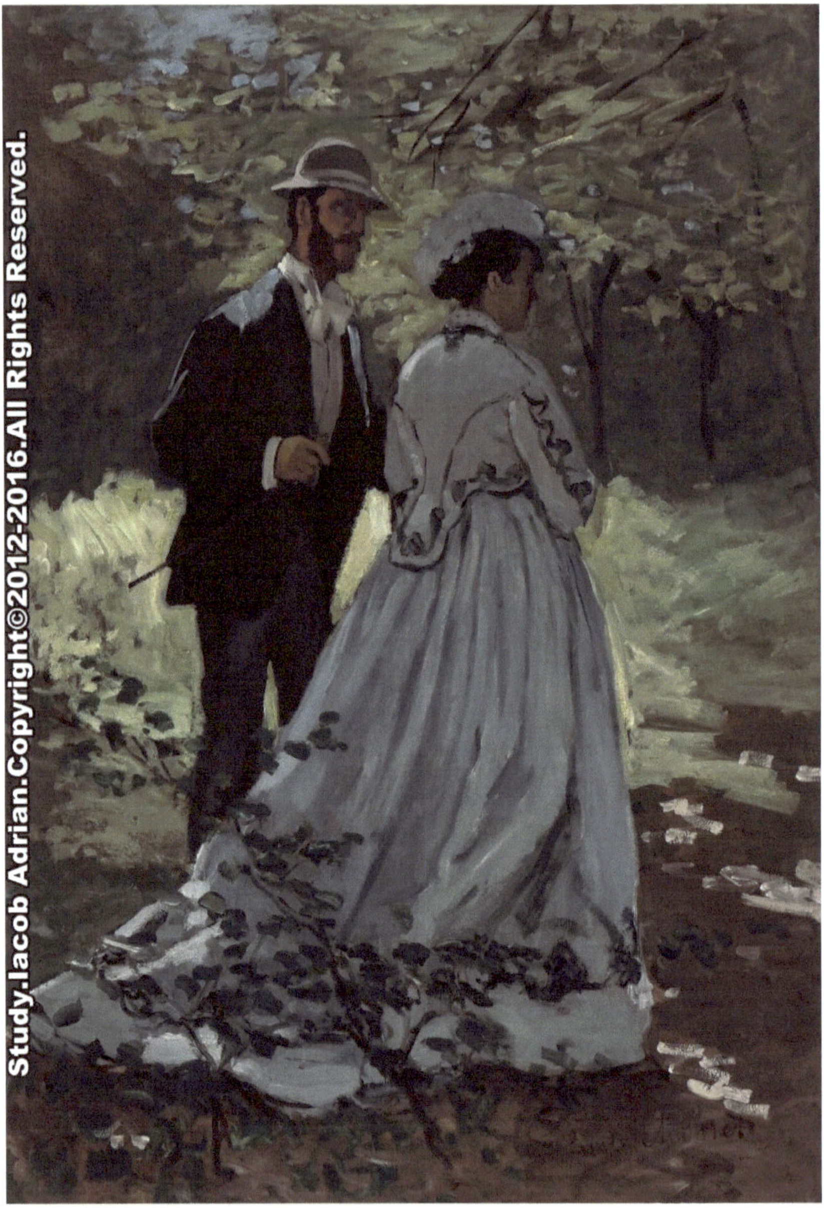

Bazille and Camille (Study for "Déjeuner sur l'Herbe")
Date : 1865

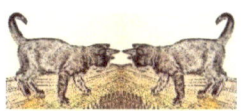

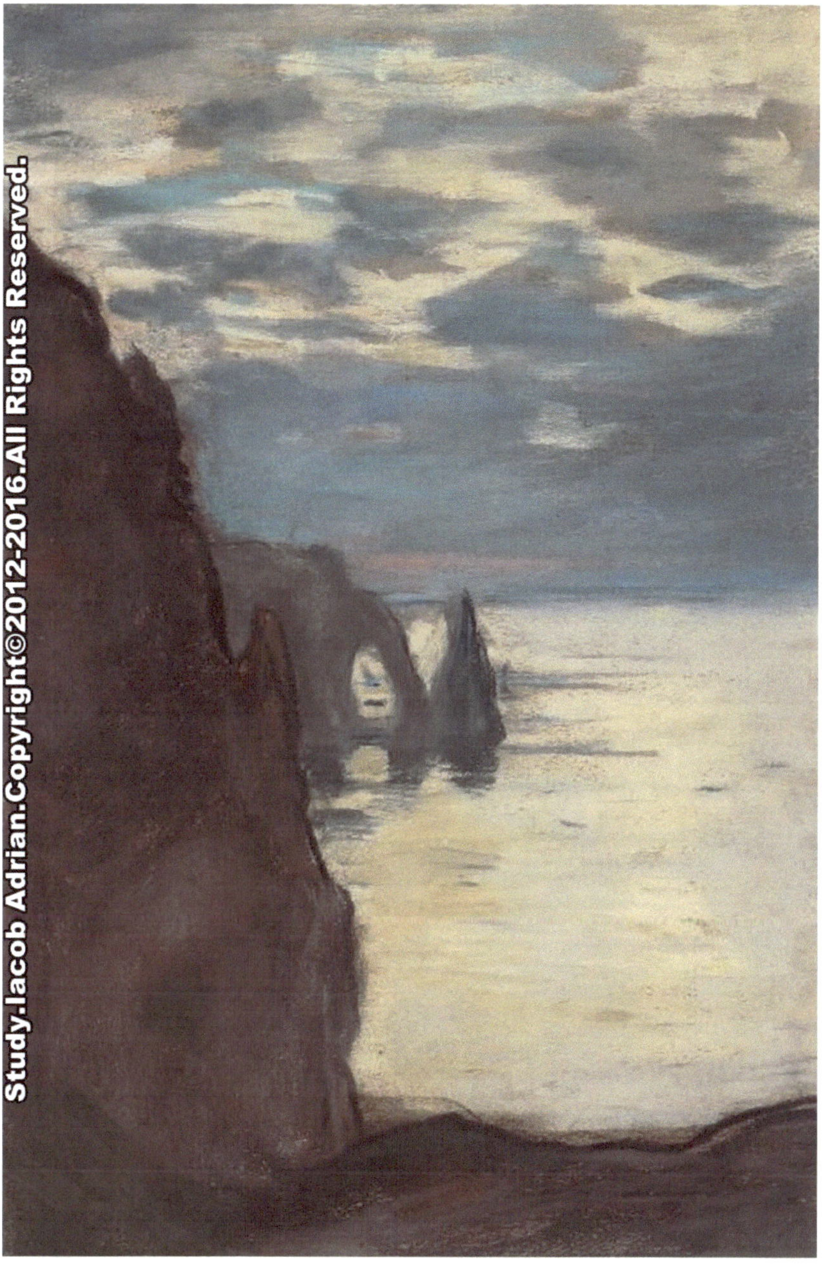

Falaise d'Etretat Aval
Date : 1890

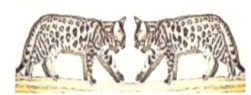

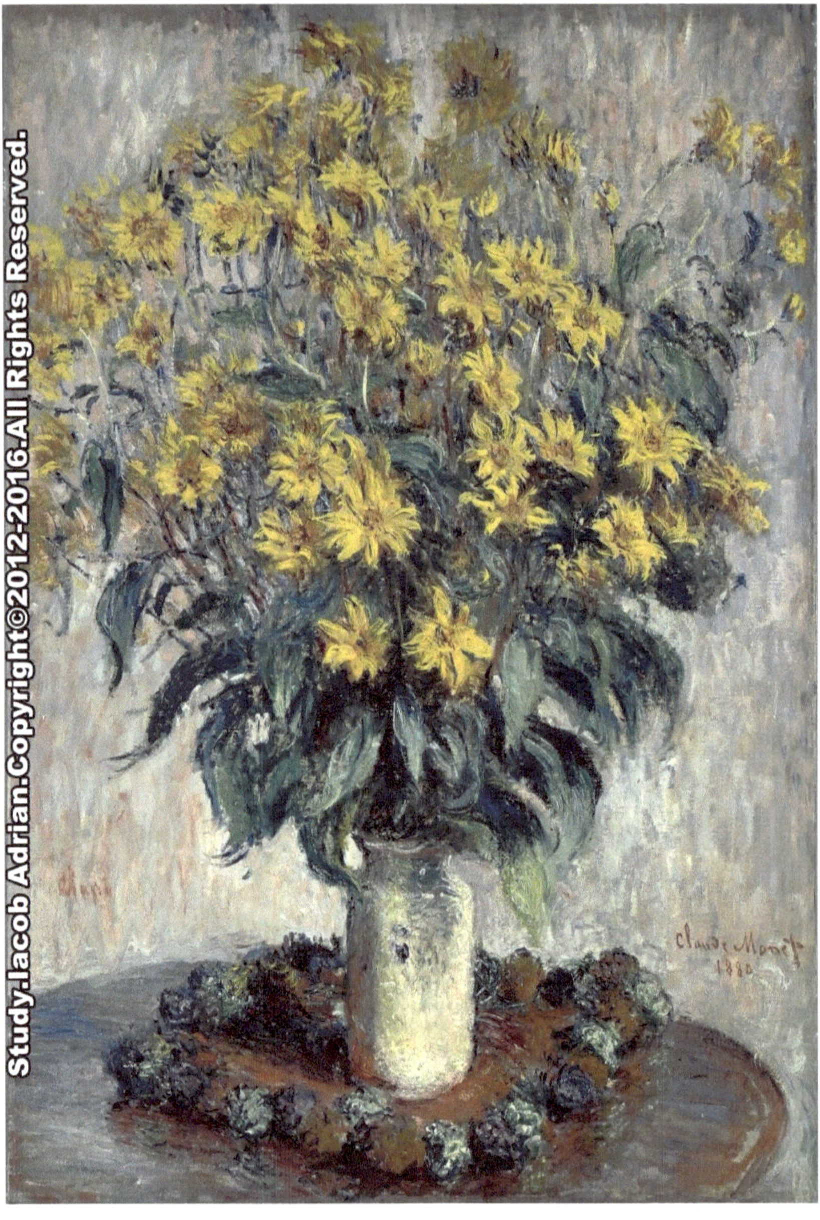

Jerusalem Artichoke Flowers
Date : 1880

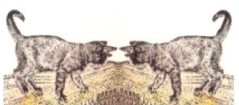

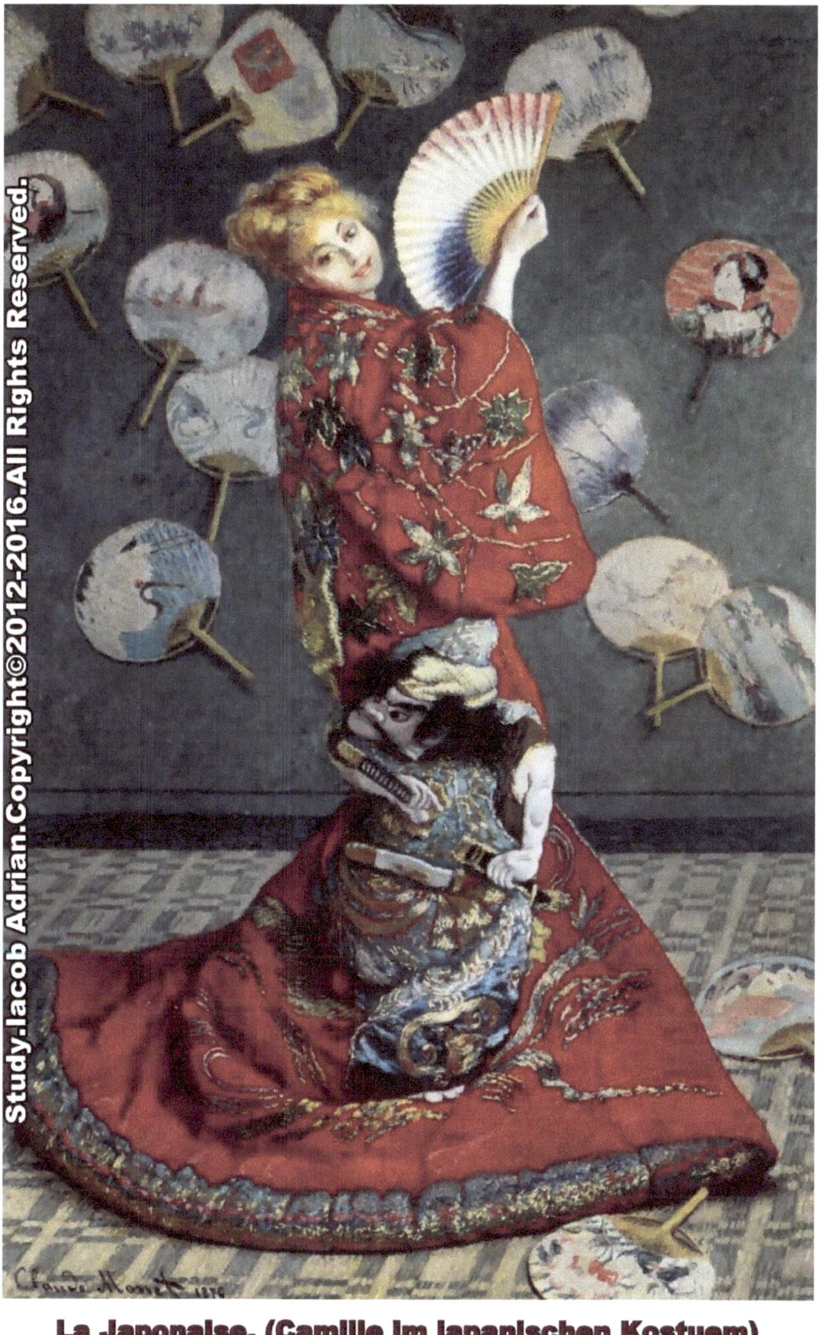

La Japonaise. (Camille im japanischen Kostuem)
Date : 1875

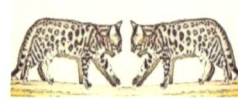

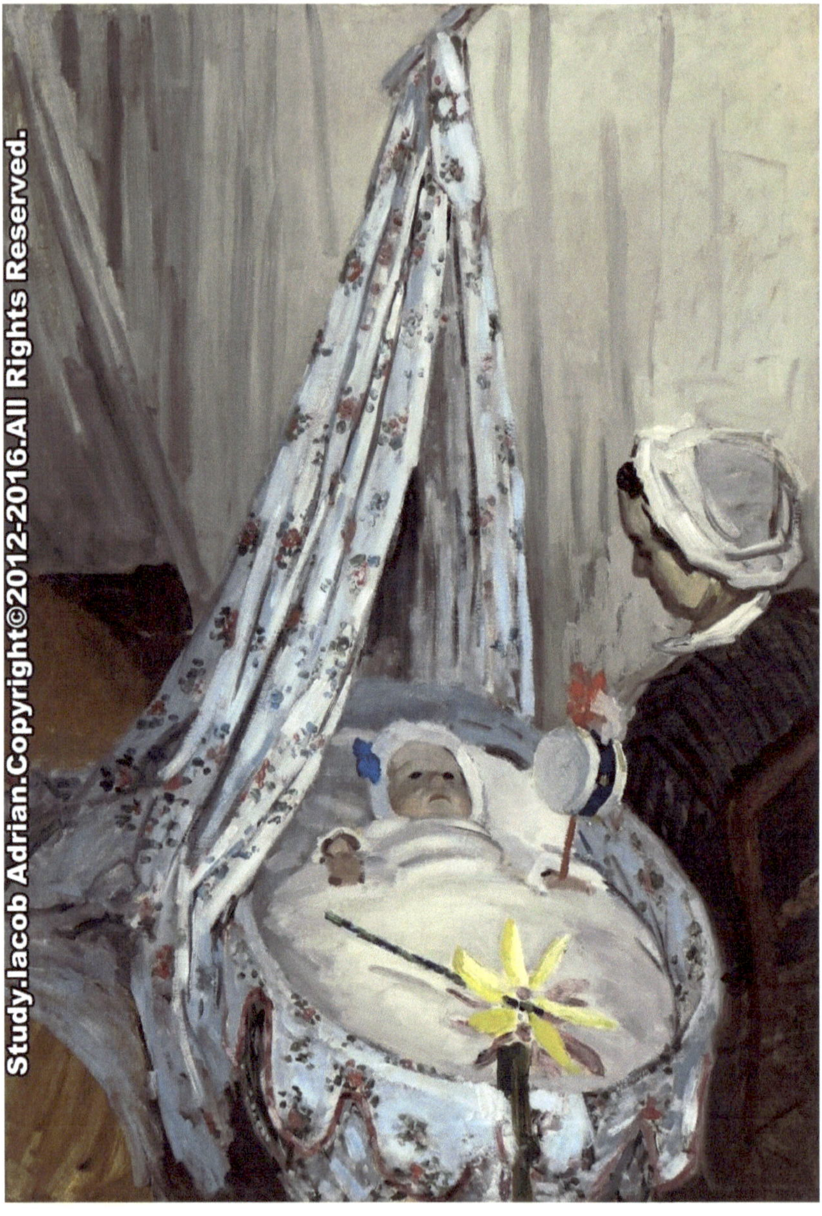

The Cradle - Camille with the Artist's Son Jean
Date : 1867

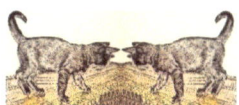

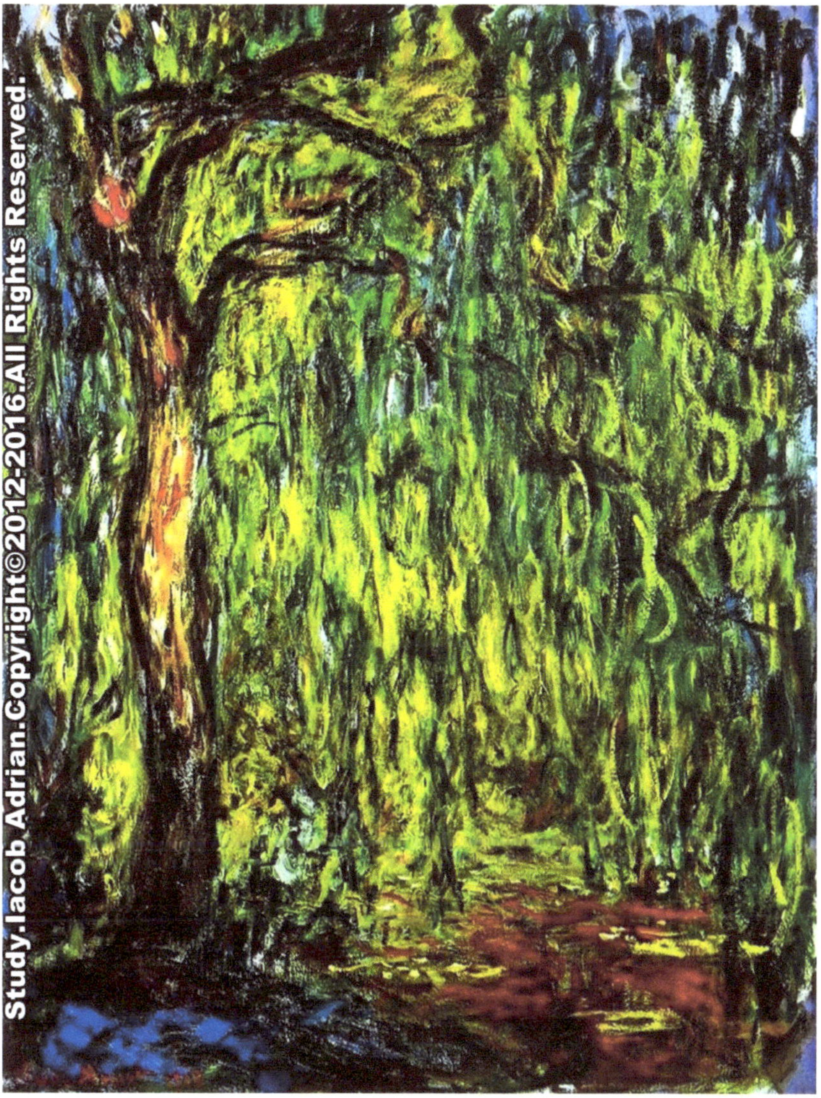

Weeping Willow
Date : n.d.

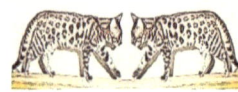

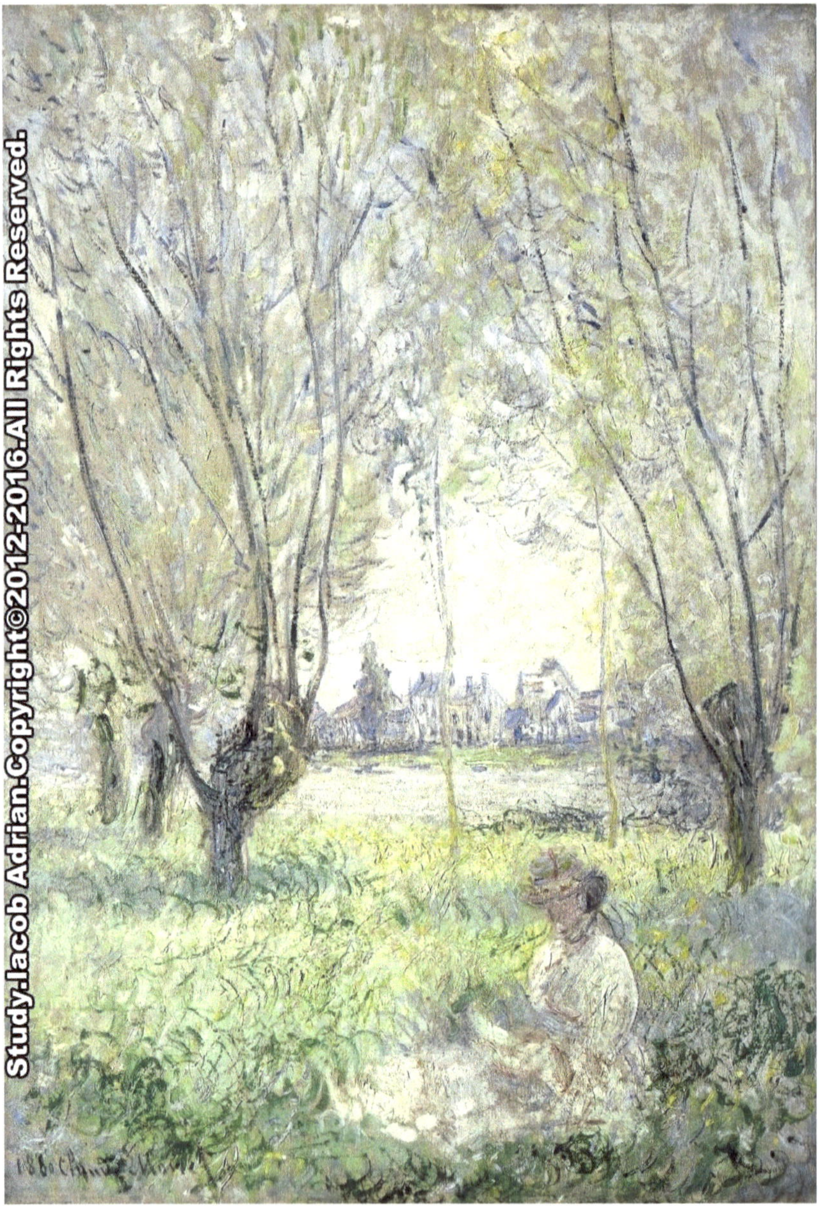

Woman Seated under the Willows
Date : circa 1880

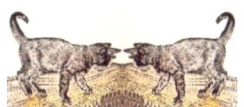

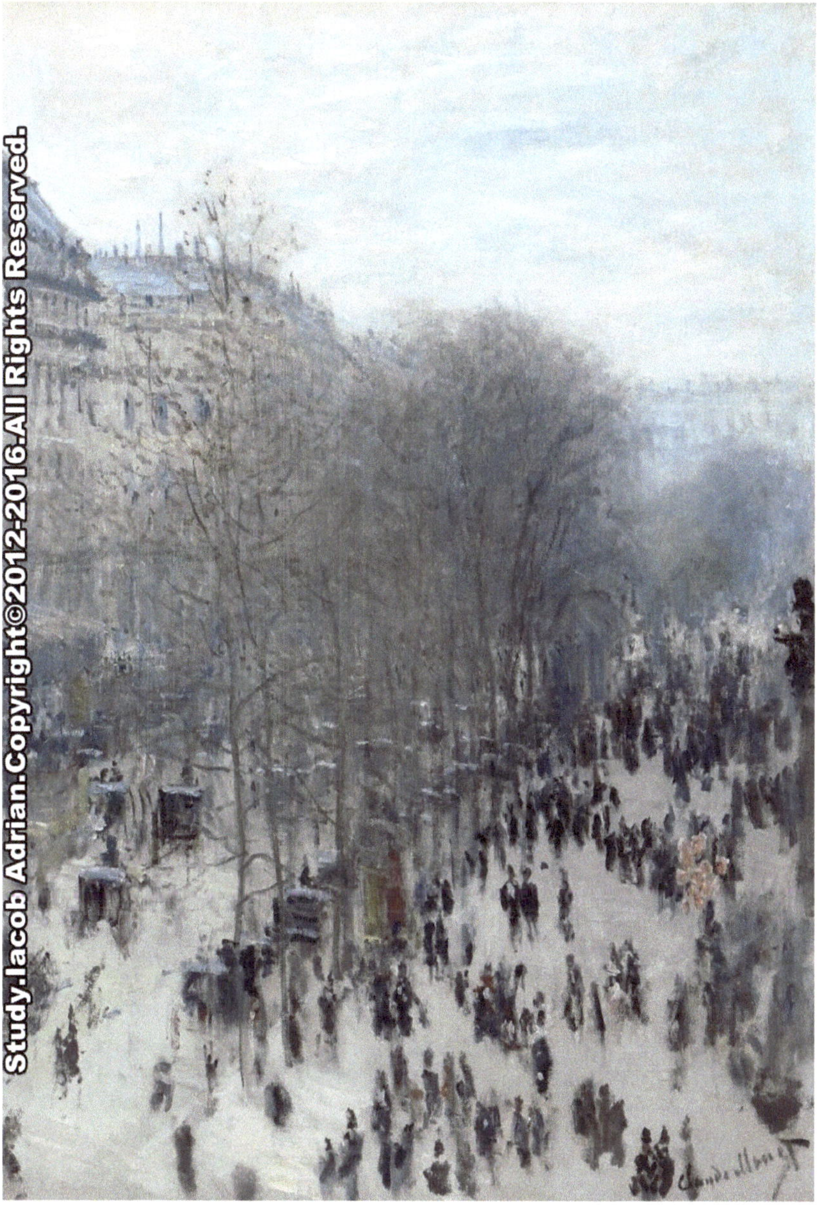

Le Boulevard des Capucines
Date : 1873-1874

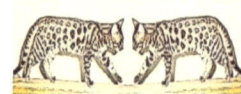

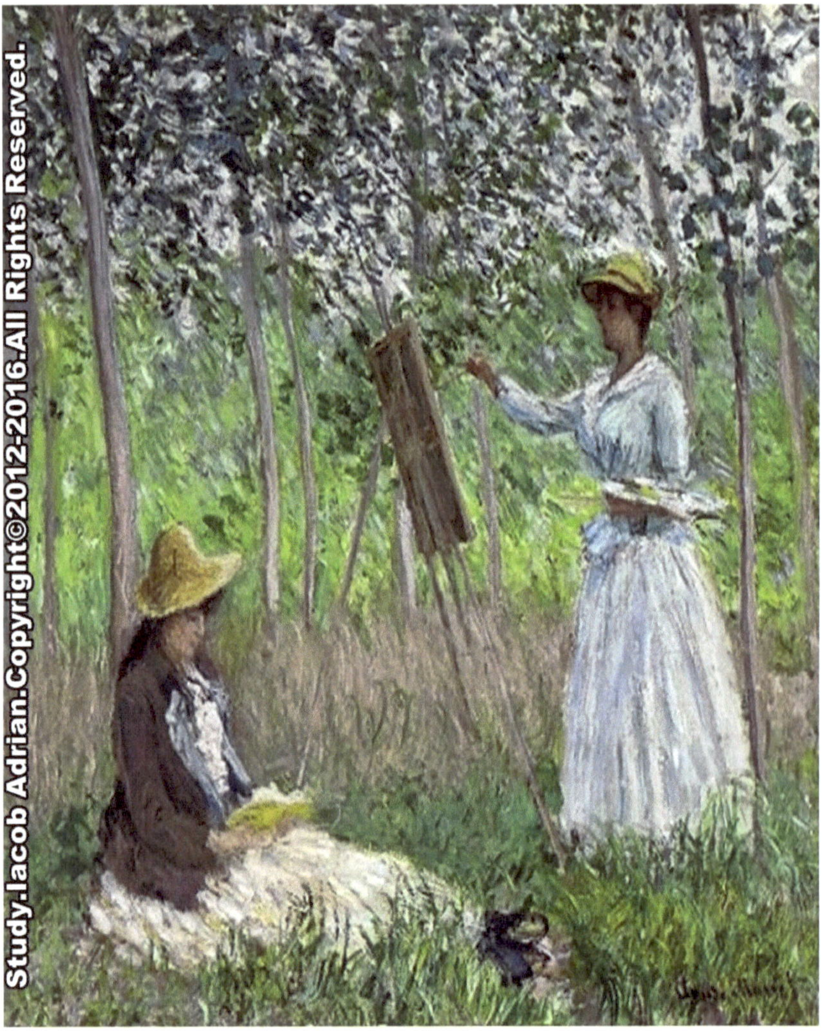

In the Woods at Giverny
Date : 1887

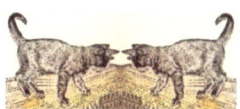

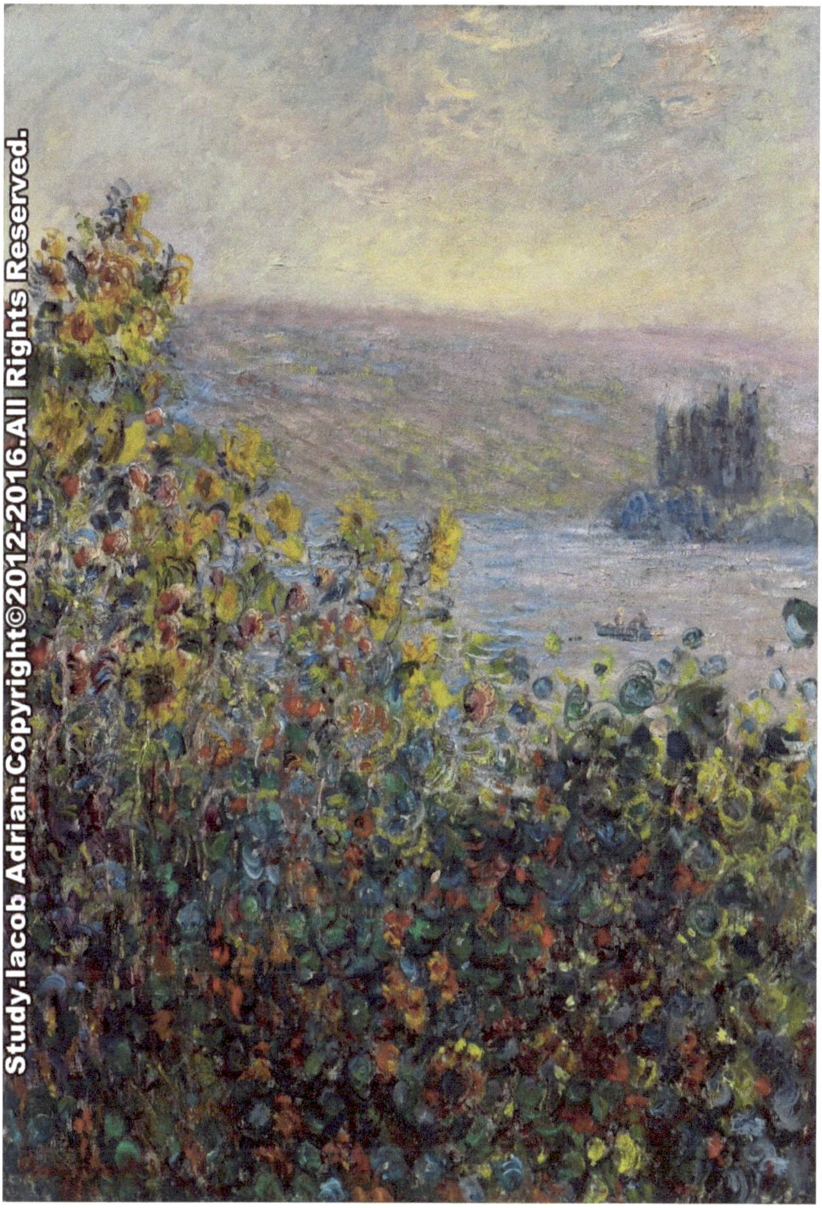

Flower Beds at Véthueil
Date : 1881

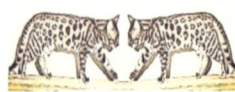

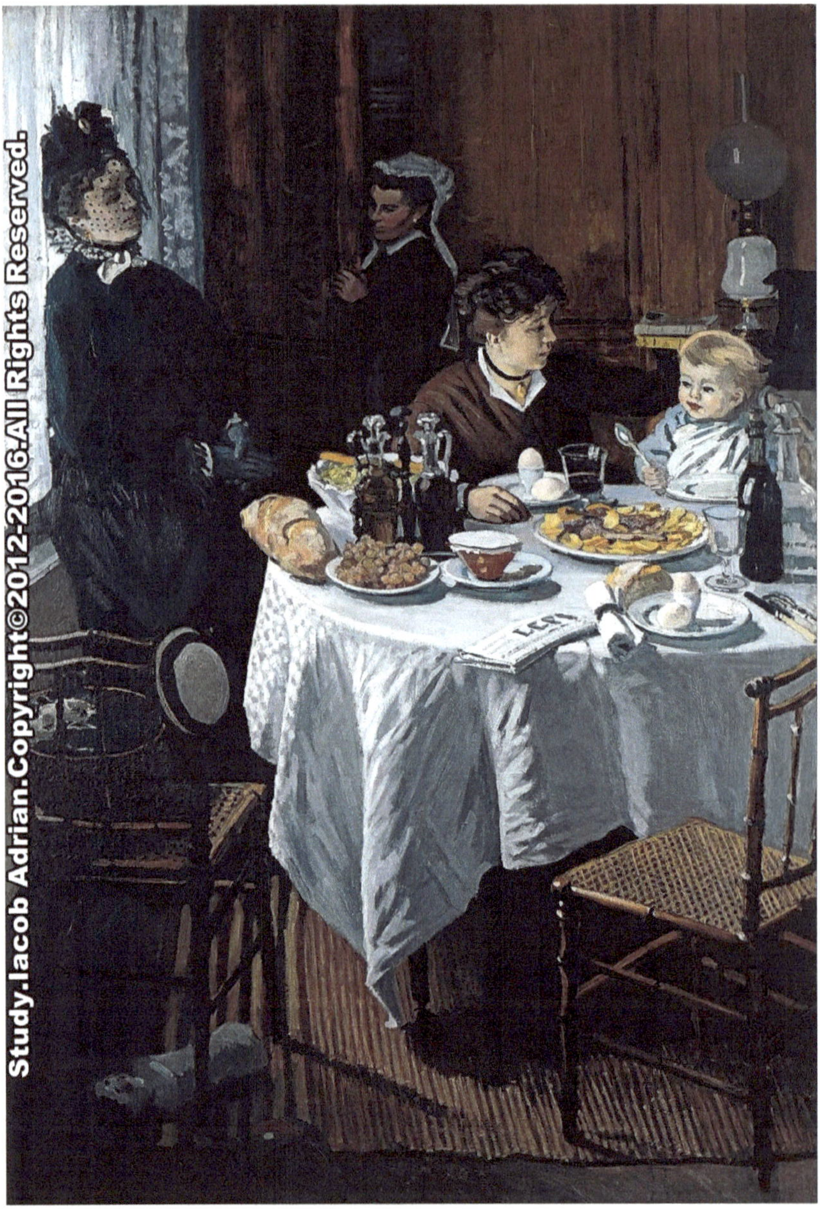

The Luncheon
Date : 1868

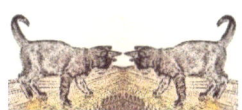

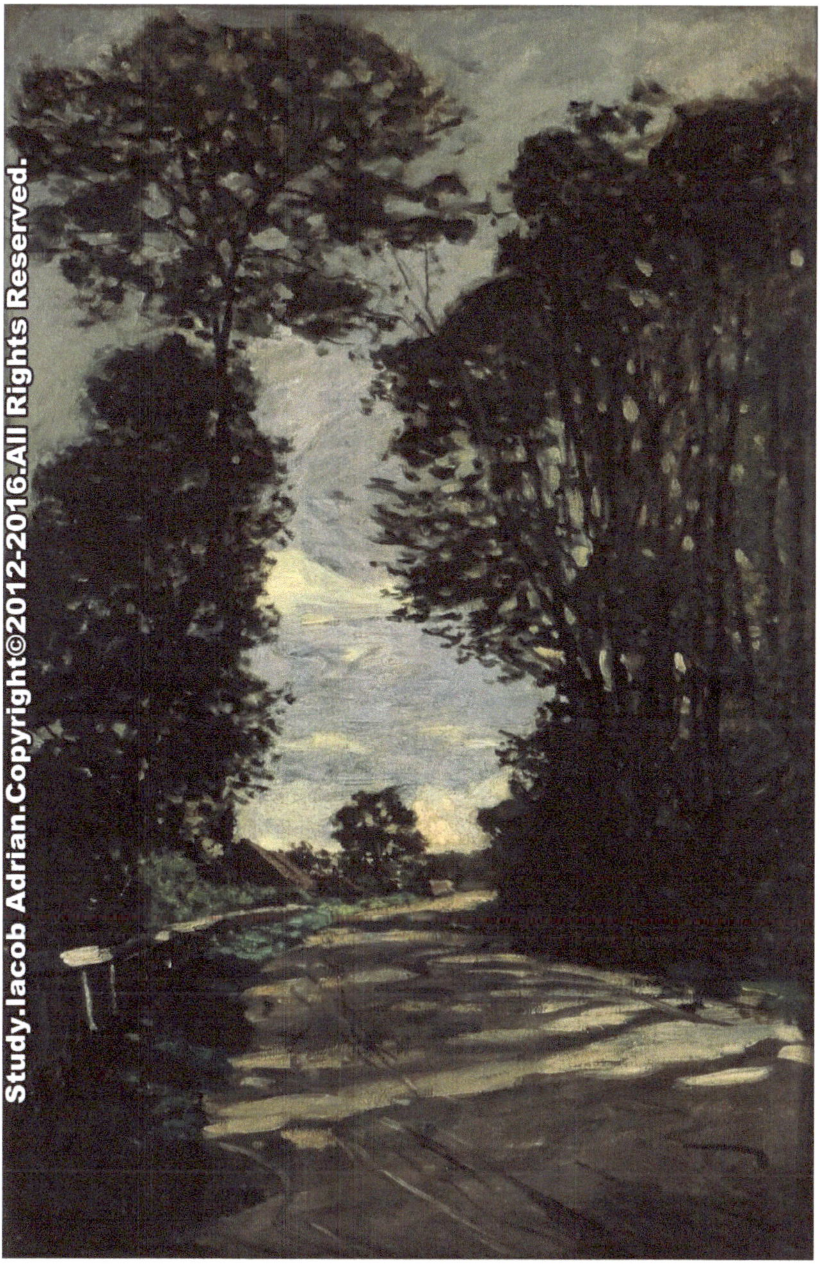

Walk (Road of the Farm Saint-Siméon)
Date : 1864

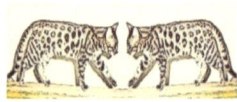

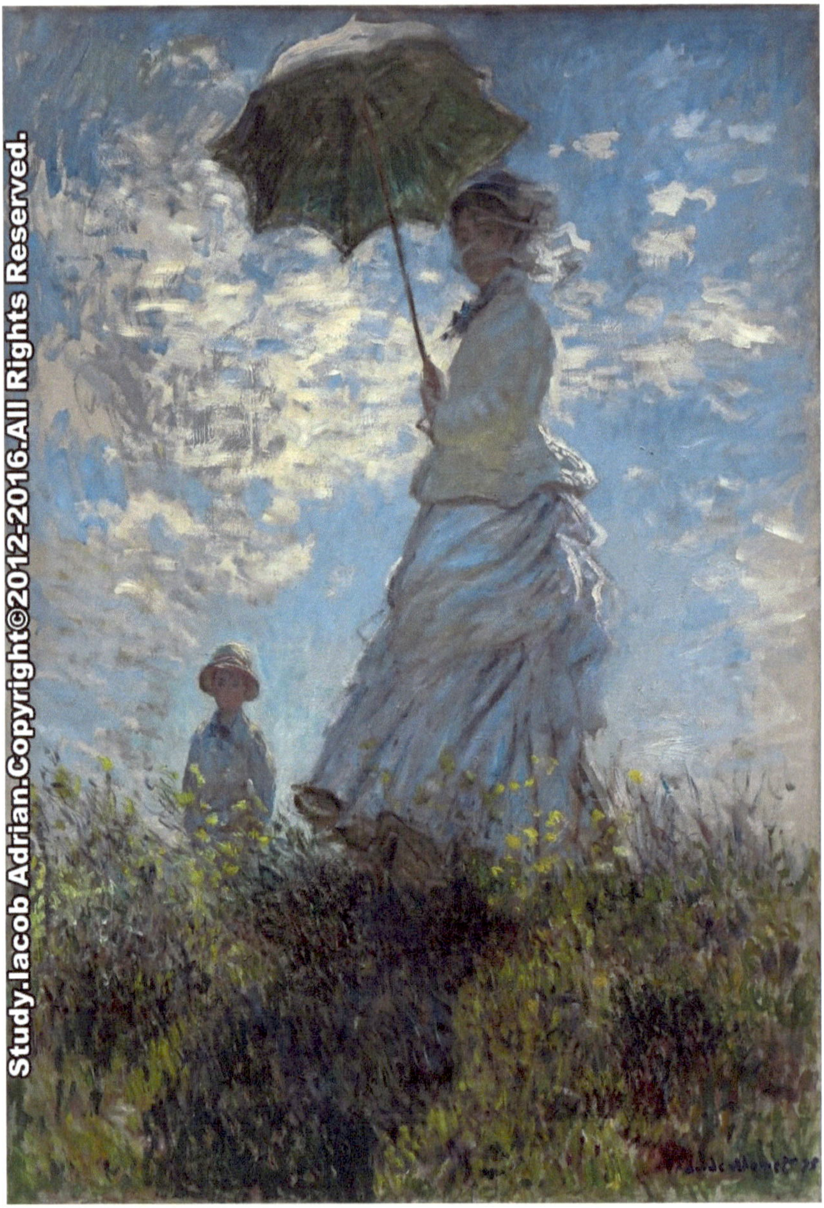

Woman with a Parasol - Madame Monet and Her Son
Date : 1875

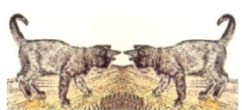

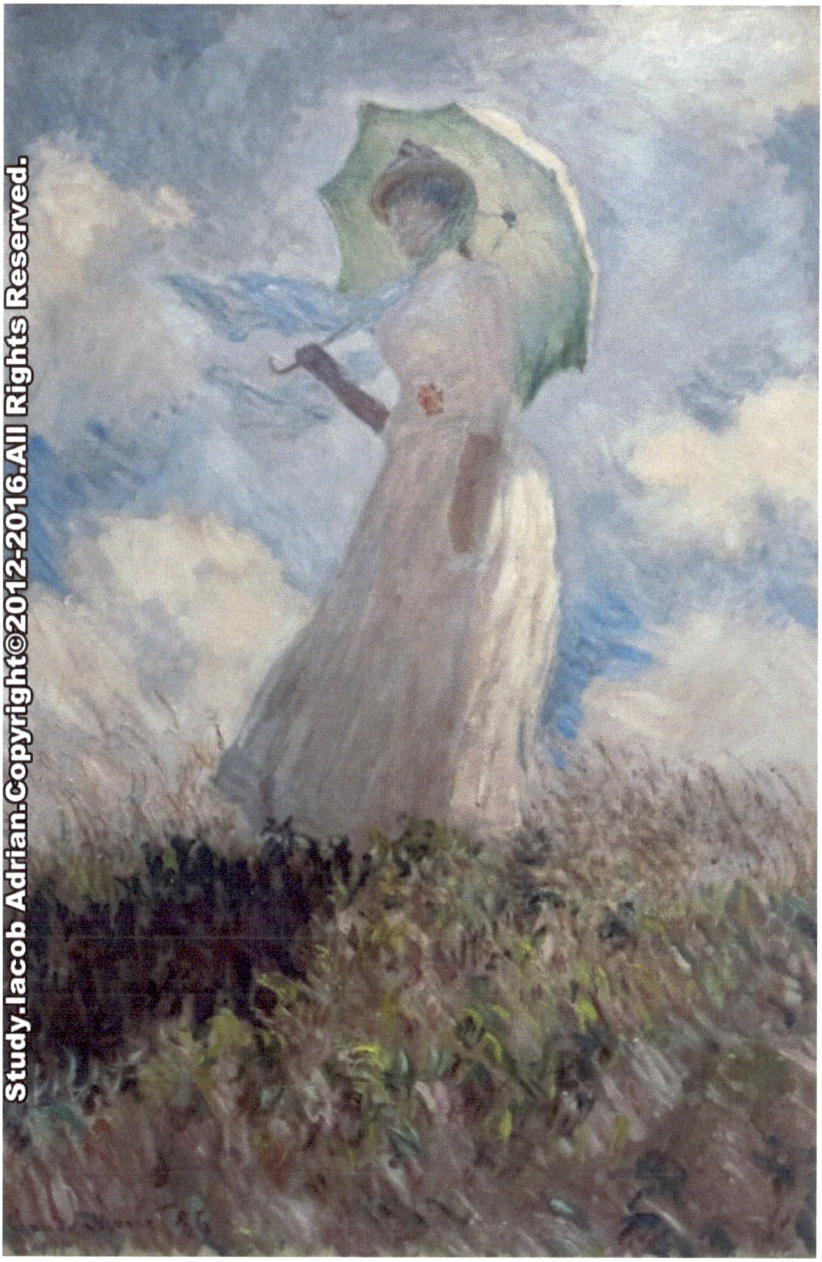

Suzanne Hoschedé, daughter of Hoschedé, second wife of Claude Monet (1868-1899)
Date : 1886

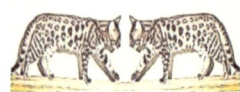

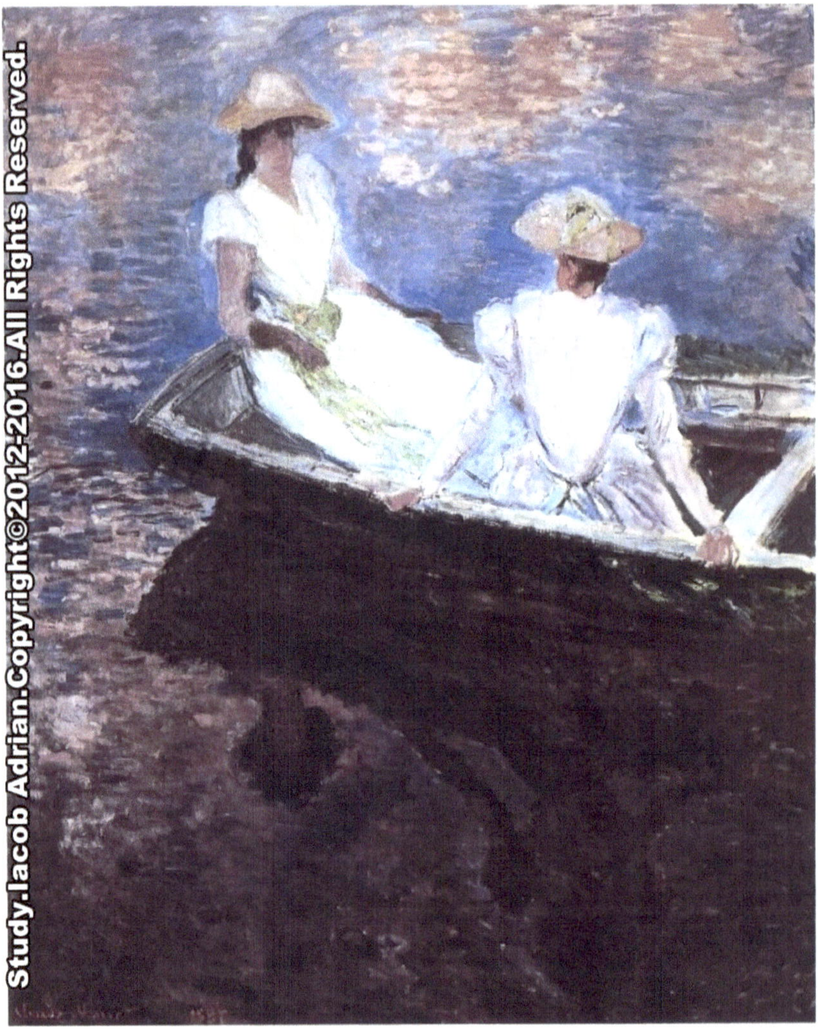

Two girls in a boat
Date : n.d.

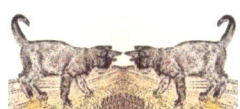

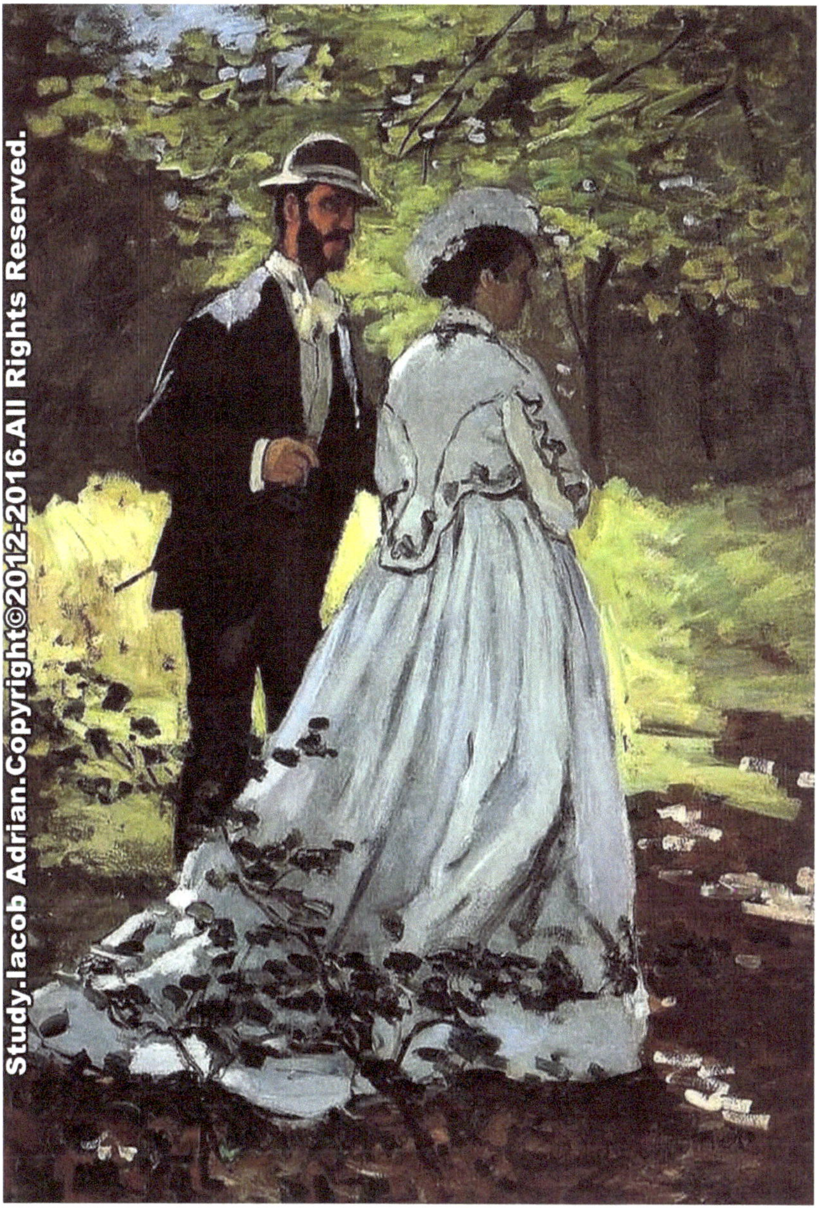

Les promeneurs
Date : 1865

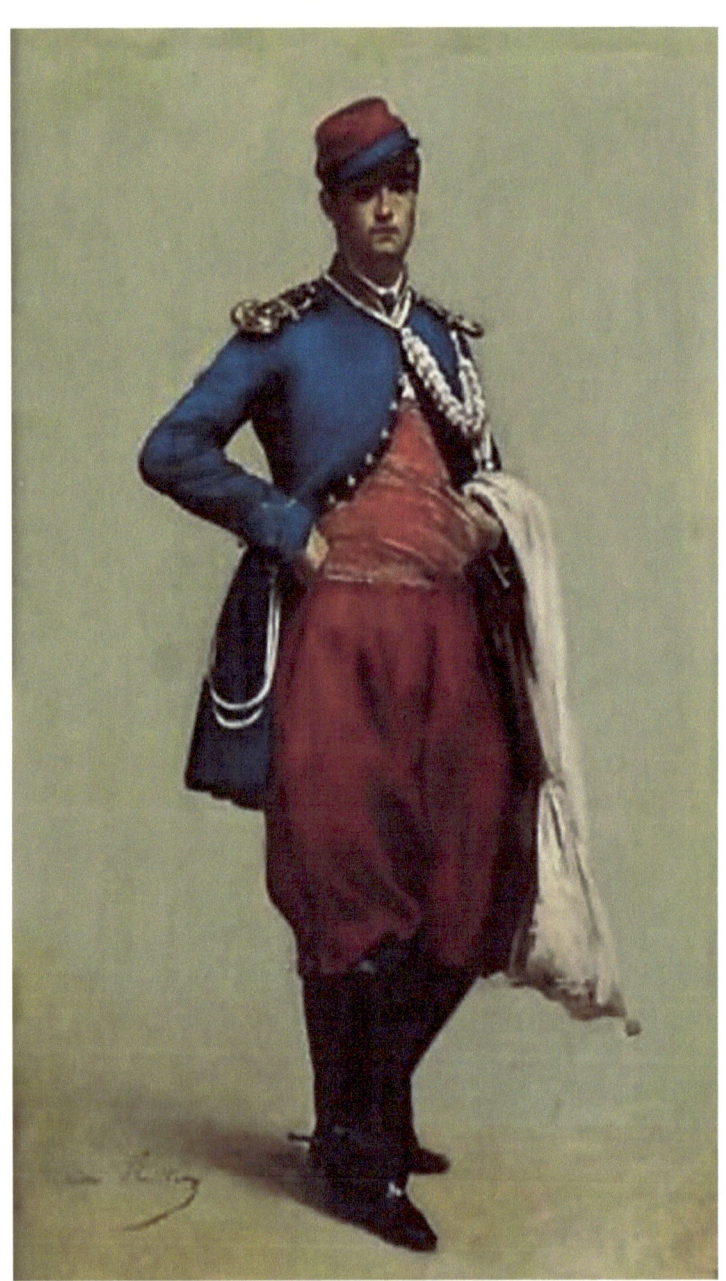

Portrait of Claude Monet in uniform by Charles Lhuillier (1824–1898)
Date : 1861

Bibliographic sources :

**Based on Paintings of
Claude Monet (1840-1926)**

and

Materials and/or elements from :
- Documentary Studies 1 collection,
- Documentary Studies 4 collection,
- Iacob Images K 4.0 collection,
Author / owner of collections : Iacob Adrian

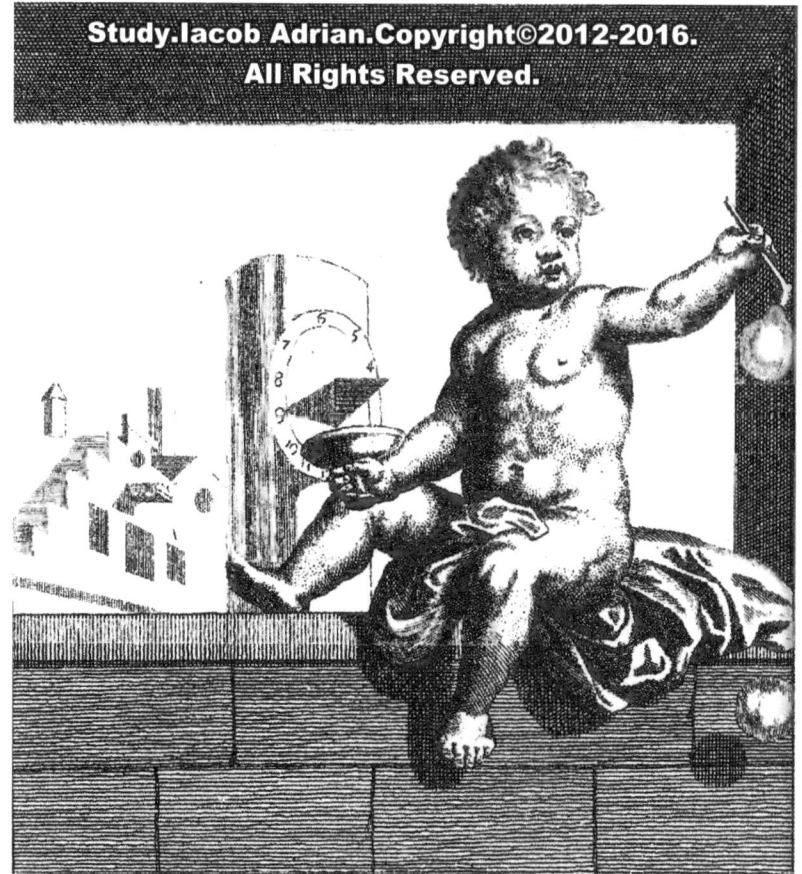

This documentary study use,
combined in various proportions,
elements from the following categories,
forms and subsets :
- fair use
- documentary
- documentary photography
- feature
- journalism
- arts journalism
- visual journalism
- photojournalism
- celebrity photography
in order to :
- employ material as the object of cultural critique ,
- quote to illustrate an argument or point ,
- use material in historical sequence,
providing independent opinion,
using photos, press articles, advertisements,
opinions of fans etc. ...

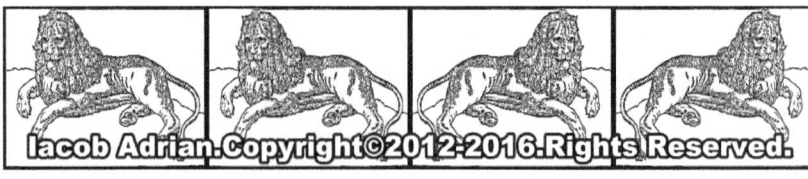

www.ingramcontent.com/pod-product-compliance
Lightning Source LLC
Chambersburg PA
CBHW041943240526
45473CB00033B/468